Step By Step Along the

PACIFIC CREST TRAIL

Tricia Andryszewski

Twenty-First Century Books
Brookfield, Connecticut

Cover photographs courtesy of Tom Stack & Associates
(top © Greg Vaughn), © Bart Smith (2nd from top, bottom, right),
SuperStock (left © John Warden)

Photographs courtesy of © Bart Smith: pp. 1 (left, right center), 3 (left,
right), 8, 9, 10, 14, 17, 23, 30, 46, 48, 55; Tom Stack & Associates: pp. 1
(left center © Greg Vaughn), 12 (© 1996 J. Lotter Gurling), 13 (© 1997 J.
Lotter Gurling), 53 (© Greg Vaughn); SuperStock: pp. 1 (right © John Warden), 22, 28 (© John Warden), 45 (© Rene Pauli), 57 (© John Warden);
Corbis-Bettmann: pp. 3 (center), 32; Photo Researchers, Inc.: p. 11
(Lawrence E. Naylor © 1986); Visuals Unlimited: pp. 19 (© John Gerlach),
34 (© Joe McDonald), 38 (© Gerald Corsi), 60 (© Joe McDonald)

Library of Congress Cataloging-in-Publication Data
Andryszewski, Tricia, 1956–
Step by step along the Pacific Crest Trail / Tricia Andryszewski.
p.   cm.
Summary: An overview of the natural history of the Pacific Crest Trail
and of historical events related to the route, an imaginary hike up the trail,
and a description of what can be seen and experienced along the way.
ISBN 0–7613–0274–3 (lib. bdg.)
1. Hiking—Pacific Crest Trail—Juvenile literature.   2. Nature study—
Pacific Crest Trail—Juvenile literature.   [1. Hiking. 2. Pacific Crest Trail.
3. Nature study.]   I. Title.
GV199.42.P3A53   1998
796.51'0979—dc21   98–7303   CIP   AC

Published by Twenty-First Century Books
A Division of The Millbrook Press, Inc.
2 Old New Milford Road
Brookfield, Connecticut 06804

CONTENTS

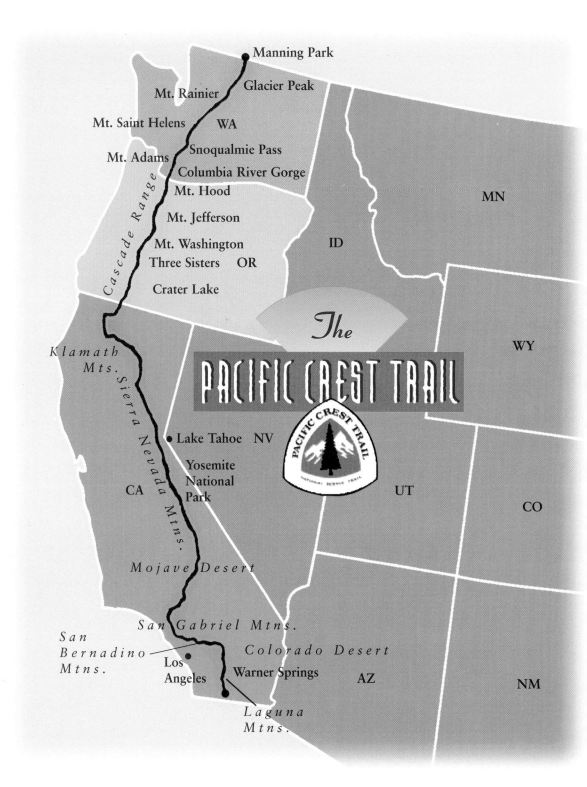

Manning Park

Glacier Peak

Mt. Rainier

Mt. Saint Helens

WA

Mt. Adams

Snoqualmie Pass

Columbia River Gorge

Mt. Hood

Mt. Jefferson

Mt. Washington

Three Sisters   OR

Crater Lake

Cascade Range

MN

Klamath Mts.

ID

WY

Sierra Nevada Mtns.

Lake Tahoe   NV

Yosemite National Park

CA

The

PACIFIC CREST TRAIL

PACIFIC CREST TRAIL

NATIONAL SCENIC TRAIL

UT

CO

Mojave Desert

San Gabriel Mtns.

San Bernadino Mtns.

Los Angeles

Colorado Desert

Warner Springs   AZ

NM

Laguna Mtns.

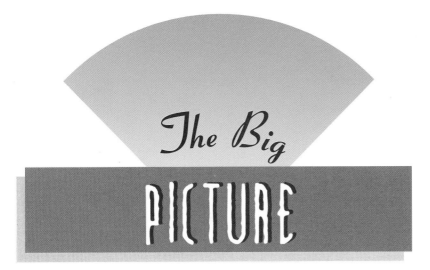

The Big PICTURE

Earthquakes! Fires! Floods! Deserts! Glaciers! Volcanoes! The Pacific Crest mountains have it all.

Earthquakes, Volcanoes, Glaciers

Many millions of years ago, two really large pieces of Earth's surface (called "plates") bumped up against each other near where the Pacific Crest Trail runs today. Rubbing against each other, the moving plates made terrible earthquakes. Pushing and shoving, the plates couldn't get past each other. The only way to go was up. And so they crumpled and thrust themselves up into mountains—huge mountain ranges made of hard, granite-type rock.

You can still see this rock sticking up out of the ground in the southern part of the Sierra Nevada mountain range. Farther north, though, most of the mountains look different.

That difference began when the land beneath the mountains in the north began to bubble and boil. Volcanoes burbled and spurted hot, melted rock (lava) from deep in the earth. The lava spread out over the northern part of the mountain range, completely covering the granite-type rock in many places. In some places, volcanoes spit out so much lava that it built itself up, layer after hardened layer, into new mountains thousands of feet tall. These are the mountains of the Cascade range, stretching from the Sierra Nevada north into Canada.

Eventually, the mountain-building earthquakes and volcanoes slowed down. (Didn't stop, though. They're still going on now, right under your feet on the Pacific Crest Trail.) The place we now call North America has, as a result of its turbulent past, several long north-to-south chains of mountains in the West, the Appalachian chain of mountains in the East, and the Great Plains in between.

About a million years ago, icy weather began to change the surface of the northern part of North America. For hundreds of years at a time during this Ice Age, summers didn't heat up enough to melt away all of the previous winters' snows. Layer after heavy layer of snow stacked up into enormous packs of ice called glaciers. These glaciers spread out over the northern, colder part of the continent like pancake batter dropped on a griddle. At one time or another, much of the northern half of North America was covered by ice hundreds or even thousands of feet thick. Because the Western mountains are so tall, and it's so cold that high up, glaciers grew farther south on these mountains than anywhere else in North America.

The glaciers grew four times during the cold centuries of the Ice Age. (In between, the glaciers retreated, melting during hundreds of years of warmer weather.) The glaciers last retreated up toward the North Pole about 10,000 years ago. Only a few remain today, on high, cold mountaintops in the Cascade Mountains.

How It All Works Today

By a few thousand years ago, most of the glaciers were gone from where the Pacific Crest Trail now runs. Serious earthquakes had become rare. Most of the volcanoes had quieted down. The landscape looked—and worked—pretty much the way it does today.

How the landscape "works" today is mainly the result of different combinations of just three basic weather facts in the West:

- **RAIN BLOWS IN FROM THE OCEAN** All of the rain and snow that falls on the Pacific Crest Trail comes from moist winds blowing east from the Pacific Ocean. These winds pick up mist rising up off the ocean and drop it in the form of rain or snow as they bump into the western mountains. As the wind goes farther east, there's less and less moisture left in it, so less and less rain or snow falls in places farther and farther from the ocean. This is why the Pacific coast forests are so moist and lush—and why the deserts farther east are so dry.

- **LOW LATITUDES ARE WARMER** Latitude is a measurement of a place's distance from the equator, the imaginary line circling the Earth midway between the North Pole and the South Pole. As hikers along the Pacific Crest Trail walk north from the Mexican border to Canada, they're walking away from the equator (where it's very hot) and toward the North Pole (where it's very cold). The weather is bathing-suit warm all year in places near the southern end of the Trail. And there are actually glaciers—permanent ice—in places near the northern end of the Trail.

- **HIGH ALTITUDES ARE COLDER** Altitude is how high a place is. Altitude is often described in "feet above sea level"—how many feet higher a place is than the level where the ocean hits the shore. Higher places, like mountaintops, tend to be colder than lower places.

Over the Pacific Crest Trail, these three facts shape nature's raw materials into dozens of different ecosystems (communities of plants and animals adapted to their local environment). The main ecosystems along the Trail include:

- **DESERT** It's too hot and dry for trees to grow in the desert. There are cactuses and a few other tough plants instead—and lizards and rattlesnakes, too.

A rattler slides out of the desert grasses.

A classic chaparral landscape

- **CHAPARRAL** A little more rain falls on chaparral than on desert, so some kinds of trees that aren't too thirsty can grow here. More common are shrubs like manzanita—a tough, bushy plant that grows thick and prickly. Hikers along the Trail in southern California walk through chaparral in two different kinds of places: in near-desert valleys and on dry mountainsides beyond where most of the rains fall.

- **WOODLAND, OR FOREST** This is the biggest ecosystem. Forests grow anywhere there's enough water for trees, clear up to the timberline on high mountaintops. Different kinds of trees grow in differ-

9

This part of the Trail is in the deep woods of Oregon.

ent forest ecosystems. In dry, hot areas of southern California, the Pacific Crest Trail passes through woodlands where California junipers and pinyon pines are the only trees that can survive. Other mixes of trees grow in different conditions along the Trail. You can see a very different kind of woodland on the very moist, mild-weathered hillsides of Oregon and Washington. There you'll find lush, thick evergreen forests dripping with mosses and ferns.

- **MOUNTAIN MEADOW** Trees do grow in mountain meadows, but not many of them; it's cold at such a high altitude, and the growing season is short. Mountain meadows are famous for their wildflowers. Because mountain summers are so short, all the flowers bloom almost at the same time.

A mountain meadow in bloom

Timberline in
the Cascade
peaks

- **ALPINE AREAS** At the top of the highest mountains
  of the Sierra Nevada, and at the top of somewhat
  shorter mountains farther north, the weather is too
  cold and too harsh for any trees to grow. Mountains
  like these are said to have a treeline or timberline. In
  the alpine (mountaintop) areas above the timberline,
  only scruffy shrubs and smaller plants can live. Some
  tiny alpine wildflowers are exquisitely beautiful.

- **GLACIERS** A few mountaintops in the northern Cascades can't support even the alpine plants—they're
  crowned with the thick ice of glaciers. The Trail mostly
  avoids crossing these glaciers' dangerous, slippery slopes.

The PCT Story

In the 1920s, hikers and other nature lovers first started to try to organize a trail running from Mexico to Canada high in the Sierra Nevada and Cascade mountains. Bits and pieces of the trail were created over the next few decades.

Then, in 1968, the U.S. Congress passed the National Trails System Act. This law set the government to work on a nationwide network of long-distance trails. The first two "scenic trails," Congress said, were to be the Appalachian Trail in the East and a Pacific Crest Trail in the West.

It took a long time to change the Pacific Crest Trail (or PCT, as it's usually abbreviated) from just a line drawn on a map to a real, walkable trail. Bit by bit, government workers and volunteers cleared and blazed the Trail. In 1993, the last section of the Trail was finally completed.

From time to time, some sections of the PCT have been moved, for several reasons. Some very dry stretches were replaced with ones where there's more water for thirsty hikers. Many sections have been moved away from land that has had all its trees cut down. A few sections have been moved to make them less dangerous for hikers or horses.

Castle Crags behind a rider on the trail

14

Yes, horses. Unlike the Appalachian Trail, the Pacific Crest Trail has been built for both hikers and equestrians (people on horseback). Hikers with pack animals, such as mules and llamas, are welcome, too.

A few hundred "thru-hikers" have walked the complete Trail—more than 2,600 miles (4,200 kilometers). Some thru-hikers make it in one unbroken journey of about four to six months. Others thru-hike the entire Trail in sections over several years. The first person to claim he had hiked the PCT in one season was eighteen-year-old Eric Ryback, in 1970. (Although he did hitch a ride in a few places, he certainly hiked *most* of the Trail that year.) Ryback's 1971 book on his PCT adventure stirred up a lot of interest in thru-hiking the Trail, and in 1972 half a dozen or so thru-hikers completed the trip. Since then, thru-hikers have included teenagers, married couples, single women, retirees, and a few equestrians. One fellow walked the whole way in sandals! Another, Bob Holtel, ran the Trail in sections over three summers—at the rate of one marathon each running day!

Southern CALIFORNIA

The Pacific Crest Trail in southern California is hot and dry. It starts at the Mexican border and runs north nearly 564 miles (908 kilometers) to the southern end of the Sierra Nevada mountain range. Along the way, it skims along ridges of the Laguna Mountains, the San Jacinto Mountains, the San Bernardino Mountains, and more. It dips briefly into the Colorado Desert and cuts across a corner of the Mojave Desert. And it passes through an almost incredible range of ecosystems, again and again.

Mexican Border to Warner Springs

The southern end of the Pacific Crest Trail is at the Mexican border, near the U.S. Border Patrol station at Campo, California, about 50 miles (80 kilometers) east of San Diego. This dry, hot country soaks up the last drops of moisture from winds blowing east from the Pacific Ocean. Just to the east of the PCT here is the burning Colorado Desert.

Monument marking
the southern
end of the Pacific
Crest Trail

The Trail soon climbs into the Laguna Mountains. Hikers who've just been sweating out 100°F (38°C) temperatures near the Mexican border in April or May often run into snowstorms in the Laguna Mountains.

Soon, though, it's back into the furnace. The Trail drops into the hot San Felipe Valley, crosses a blistering section of the Colorado Desert, then heads along the San Felipe Hills to Warner Springs.

17

Warner Springs Through the San Jacinto Mountains to San Gorgonio Pass

Mineral-rich hot water bubbles up out of the ground at Warner Springs. Native Americans bathed in this hot spring centuries ago. The Western adventurer Kit Carson visited in 1846 and a few years later, stagecoach passengers stopped here overnight on long east-west journeys. Today it's a privately owned spa. North of Warner Springs, Trail hikers zigzag through dry chaparral on a checkerboard of government-owned pieces of land, heading for the San Jacinto Mountains.

The San Jacinto Mountains are the first truly high mountains crossed by PCT hikers heading north from Mexico. At the northern end of the San Jacinto Mountains, the Trail drops almost 8,000 feet (2,400 meters) to the hot, dry San Gorgonio Pass. On the way down from the mountains, the PCT passes through several ecosystems—from cool pine forest to desert.

It's not unusual for hikers in grassy and brushy places along the Trail to pull *dozens* of ticks off clothes and skin

Ticks can be tiny and hard to see. Your best defense against them is to wear long sleeves with snug cuffs and long pant legs tucked into socks. (It's hard for ticks to get to your skin that way.) Tick repellent spray can help. Checking yourself carefully for ticks at least once a day in tick country is a must.

Although rattlesnakes live in many places along the Trail, they are most common in hot, dry places. The most feared and dangerous snake along the Trail is the Mojave green rattlesnake.

Rattlesnakes would much rather leave you alone than bite you. If you can avoid surprising a snake, the snake will avoid you. So: Watch your step, and don't step on a snoozing rattler! Don't put your hand into places where a snake might be hiding from the heat of the day. If you do see (or hear) a rattler, LEAVE IT ALONE and walk away from it, giving it plenty of room. Anybody who does get bitten by a poisonous snake should stay calm and get to a hospital as soon as possible for a shot of antivenin (a drug that acts against the poison).

A rattlesnake snoozing in the sun. They are well camouflaged, so keep your eyes open!

19

Where there are rattlers, there are sure to be mice.

"A tiny mouse runs across my face, then trots off to nibble on some leftover trail mix crumbs. After a series of stunts, including double and triple somersaults, tailspins, and nosedives (all on a full stomach!) my visitor, using my chin as a diving board, scurries off into the forest as I nod off to sleep."

THRU-RUNNER
BOB HOLTEL

Bob Holtel ran the Pacific Crest Trail in 110 running days plus 46 rest days over three summers in the 1980s.

in a day! These flat little bloodsuckers can carry such serious diseases as Rocky Mountain spotted fever and Lyme disease. Fortunately, it's very rare to find ticks with these diseases near the PCT.

San Gorgonio Pass Through the San Bernardino Mountains to Cajon Canyon

The San Gorgonio Pass is a wide, sandy, windy gap between the San Jacinto Mountains to the south and the San Bernardino Mountains to the north. Standing at the low point in the pass, you can look up and see mountains towering 9,000 feet (2,700 meters) above you, north and south of the pass, just a few miles apart.

Beyond San Gorgonio Pass, the PCT climbs northward into the San Bernardino Mountains—a popular playground for hikers from San Diego and Los Angeles. The Trail runs, for more than 100 miles (160 kilometers), along the entire length of this mountain range. Hikers heading north first go through more chaparral, then a sparse and dry woodland where short pinyon pines are the star attraction. (Native Americans collected pinyon pine nuts and ground them into a rich and tasty flour.) As the Trail climbs higher, the climate grows cooler, the soil moister. Jeffrey pines and incense cedars—trees that need a little more water than the pinyon pines—grow here. Where the Trail reaches about 7,000

The sticky, oily juice of the poison oak plant can give your skin an ugly, itchy, painful, oozy rash that makes you totally miserable. Like poison ivy, all parts of the poison oak plant are dangerous to touch—even bare woody stems. Poison oak grows along the Trail in many, many places in California below an altitude of 5,000 feet (1,500 meters). It's unusual, though, to see poison oak along the Pacific Crest Trail in Oregon and Washington, except for stretches near the Columbia River.

feet (2,100 meters) above sea level, a full-blown forest grows. Higher still, patches of winter snow remain unmelted well into early summer. In this near-alpine ecosystem, only cold-tolerant, stunted-looking trees survive.

Rainfall as well as altitude shapes the ecosystems in these mountains. The amount of rain varies a lot from one side of a mountain range to the other. Along the PCT near Big Bear Lake, for example, at more than 7,000 feet (2,134 meters) above sea level, well above the desert floor, you might expect to find forest. Instead, there's more dryland pinyon pine there because the Mojave Desert side of the mountain range gets little rain.

The Trail follows the San Bernardino mountains westward through the upper part of their range, then veers north to Cajon Canyon, where it passes beneath a six-lane highway—U.S. 15. Cajon Canyon runs along the famous

This aerial view of the San Andreas fault shows both new and old scars caused by the shifting plates.

San Andreas fault. Earthquakes rattle Los Angeles, San Francisco, or other places along California's Pacific Coast whenever one piece of the earth's crust moves against another along this long fault line.

Cajon Canyon Through the San Gabriel Mountains to Agua Dulce

Beyond Cajon Canyon, the Trail climbs steeply into the San Gabriel Mountains. Here it soon reaches Mount Baden-Powell, 9,399 feet (2,865 meters) above sea level, named after the founder of the Boy Scouts. Limber pines grow along the windswept side trail to the summit of Mount Baden-Powell. Plant experts believe that these gnarled, twisted pines may be as much as 2,000 years old!

The steep San Gabriel Mountains' wild and rough terrain is diverse: There is everything from hot, dry chaparral to near-alpine icy mountaintops. Most of the PCT through these mountains, though, winds through shady

The wild and wonderful shape of a limber pine

"A sleek, fleet-winged hawk swoops down from nowhere, searching for prey. Its sharp eyes constantly scan the ground below, and, in an abrupt move, the hawk slams its wings in reverse to stop in midair. It hovers a moment, then dives toward my torso, and at the last moment pulls up short, swishing past and upward again without losing speed. It perches in a treetop and squawks mercilessly. . . . The message is clear. I quickly leave the domain of this animated fighter plane."

THRU-RUNNER
BOB HOLTEL

forest, where pine needles cushion the ground beneath your feet.

Beyond the San Gabriel Mountains, the Trail dips down into Soledad Canyon, then over a ridge into Escondido Canyon, then on to the little town of Agua Dulce.

Agua Dulce Through the Mojave Desert to Tehachapi Pass

From Agua Dulce, the PCT winds northwest nearly 50 miles (80 kilometers) through hot chaparral and cooler, wooded hillsides to Liebre Mountain. There, the Trail turns northeast, dropping down out of the mountains to cross Antelope Valley—the western arm of the awesome Mojave Desert.

Air temperatures reach as high as 120°F (49°C) in the Mojave Desert, and the air is dry as sun-bleached bones. In this kind of dry heat, hikers may need to drink as much as two to three gallons of water a day!

Why does the Trail cross the Mojave Desert, instead of continuing along the Tehachapi Mountains to the Sierra Nevada? The original plan was to have the PCT stick to the mountaintops here. (It is, after all, the Pacific *Crest* Trail.) But much of the Tehachapi Mountains is privately owned, part of the huge Tejon Ranch, and the ranch's owners didn't want the Trail to run across their property.

Some of the Trail's path through the Mojave Desert follows the Los Angeles Aqueduct, a huge underground pipe that carries mountain water to the city. Thirsty hikers used to dip into this underground river to refill their water bottles—until maintenance crews cemented over the aqueduct's access hole covers.

The Trail passes through stands of Joshua trees near the edge of the desert. These bizarre, oddly branched "trees" are actually not trees at all—they belong to the lily family. Mormon pioneers in the 1800s thought they looked like the Old Testament prophet Joshua, pointing the way to the Mormons' new homeland at the Great Salt Lake. And that's how they got their name.

Beyond Cottonwood Creek, the PCT leaves the drylands behind. Joshua trees and creosote bushes begin to give way to low-growing junipers as the Trail climbs into the northern section of the Tehachapi Mountains. Soon, pinyon pines line the Trail again. After passing its high point in the Tehachapi Mountains—6,280 feet (1,914 meters)—the Trail drops gently down to cross Oak Creek at a grove of white oak trees. From here, the Trail heads toward Tehachapi Pass—the end of the Tehachapi Mountains.

"It's so bright out here! The intense light is not just from direct sunlight, but is reflected off the bright sand. There's no dark place to cool your eyes. Same with the heat. . . . There are no trees to shield you [from the sun]. Then the land absorbs the heat, and it rises from beneath you. Double dose!"

THRU-HIKER
CINDY ROSS

Cindy Ross thru-hiked the PCT over two summers, south to north.

25

Southern and HIGH SIERRA

The next stretch of the Pacific Crest Trail is one of the most exciting, and popular. In just under 450 action-packed miles (729 kilometers), the Trail marches over the southern Sierra to magnificent Mount Whitney, then onto the John Muir Trail and up the High Sierra to Sonora Pass. Prime hiking season for the Sierra is July and August, when the mountain weather is deliciously cool and mild.

Tehachapi Pass to Walker Pass

At Tehachapi Pass, northbound hikers on the Pacific Crest Trail leave the Tehachapi Mountains behind and go up, up, up into the Sierra Nevada. (Geographers say the little Tehachapis are actually the southern tail of the mighty Sierra Nevada mountain range, but most hikers don't see it that way.)

In just 84 miles (135 kilometers), hikers along this section of the Trail pass through a wild variety of landscapes. On its way to the Piute Mountains, the Trail climbs past

> "Atop the Kern Plateau . . . the forest is a hospitable place, easy and gentle for living. Summers are pleasantly warm and there is plenty of moisture. Deer graze. Meadows fill with wildflowers. . . .
>
> "Ponderosa pines dot the forest. They are big trees, with yellow-pink, deeply grooved bark. . . . Beneath the trees are carpets of apricot-colored needles.
>
> "We've noticed a definite change in the daily weather pattern since we climbed the plateau. Brilliant blue skies greet us in the morning. As the day progresses, cottony cumulus clouds build. By midafternoon thunder rumbles, and we're driven under cover. Rain and frozen ice balls beat the earth."
>
> THRU-HIKER
> CINDY ROSS

Joshua trees and junipers into a landscape of pinyon pines and oak. In the Piutes, tall, cool Jeffrey pines line the Trail. Next, the Trail drops back into desert, then climbs up again into more pinyon pines. All along the way, there are terrific clear views of distant mountains, vast deserts, and deep valleys.

Walker Pass to Mount Whitney

This section of the Trail goes through the Southern Sierra's Kern Plateau. In keeping with its name, the Pacific Crest Trail here keeps to the highlands, following along a section of the twisting and turning, wild and beautiful South Fork Kern River. Farther up the Trail is Monache Meadow, the largest meadow in the entire Sierra Nevada mountain range.

At higher elevations, the Trail runs on exposed, rocky land where the climate is harshly windy and cold. Here are groves of stunted, twisted foxtail pines.

Near the northern end of this section, the Trail enters Sequoia National Park. (The famous giant sequoia trees that give this park its name are well down the western slopes of the mountains, far from the PCT.) This is black bear country, and campers should hang their food well out of reach of any bears looking for a nighttime snack.

Finally, at the very end of this section, just past Mount Guyot, a long side trail off the PCT leads up the awesome Mount Whitney.

Black bears share the Trail with you—make sure you give them plenty of room.

"Climbing out of Crabtree Meadow [on the way up Mount Whitney], we see life diminishing with each step. Lodgepole [pines] reach only eight to ten feet [2.5 to 3 meters] high, growing to the level of the packed snow. Avalanches will roar over and behead anything taller. As we climb higher still, we find stunted whitebark pines scattered in patches, misshapen by the cold, harsh winds. . . . You can tell which way the wind blows, all the trees lean in that direction. They are gnarled and stooped, like old men and women."

Far beyond timberline, at the top of Mount Whitney, jagged mountains extend as far as you can see. The sky is a shade of deep, dark blue that you will never see at lower elevations. There's nothing green anywhere. Just steel gray granite and snow. . . .

"It seems to us that there is no higher place in all the world. This is it! The top of the earth. The next flight up is heaven."

THRU-HIKER
CINDY ROSS

Mount Whitney

At 14,492 feet (4,400 meters) above sea level, the top of Mount Whitney is the highest point in the United States south of Alaska. The side trail from the PCT to Mount Whitney climbs nearly 4,000 feet (1,219 meters) in about 8.5 miles (14 kilometers). The air is thin at this high altitude. Many hikers get physically sick from being up so high, and everybody gasps for breath in the thin air. Weather at the bare, rocky, icy summit is harsh and dangerous. Afternoon lightning storms can be deadly; with no trees at the summit to attract the lightning, hikers standing upright are prime targets.

"The view from the top of Mount Whitney is what dreams are made of. Certainly what posters are made of. Intricately patterned worlds of rock and snow confront the eye at every turn, as if I were sitting inside a mountain kaleidoscope."

THRU-HIKER
DAVID GREEN

David Green thru-hiked the Trail in one summer, south to north.

But on a clear day—what a view at the top! You can see all the major peaks of the Sierra Nevada. Sometimes you can even see as far back down the Trail as the San Bernardino Mountains, hundreds of miles to the south.

Mount Whitney to Tuolumne Meadows

North of Mount Whitney, the PCT joins up with the famous John Muir Trail for most of its 175-mile (282-kilometer) stretch through

Finally! The view from the top of Mount Whitney

30

"July is the hottest month in the Sierra. The greatest snow melt occurs then and all but the highest peaks wake up and come alive. . . .

"With only six to eight weeks to complete their cycle, the flowers bloom furiously. After only a few days, it seems, the ground is bursting with their color. No time is wasted."

THRU-HIKER
CINDY ROSS

"I didn't get much sleep tonight; mice were attacking my pack. I could even catch them with my flash-light peeking around my pack, but knock around as much as I might, I'd still hear them five minutes later ripping holes in my food bags. I'd picture pow-dered milk spilling all over the inside of the pack, and then I'd get furious. These guys just won't quit."

THRU-HIKER
TOM MARSHBURN

Nineteen-year-old Tom Marshburn started his PCT thru-hike at the northern end, in Canada. He completed it five months later, at the Mexican border.

the spectacular High Sierra. The Trail soon climbs to 13,180 feet (4,018 meters) above sea level at Forester Pass—the highest point on the entire Pacific Crest Trail.

The High Sierra has everything a mountain hiker could ask for: glorious mountain peaks, thousands of sparkling mountain lakes, hundreds of miles of protected wilderness. Even the weather is surprisingly mild for such high and rugged mountains, and in the summer the sun usually shines most hours of the day.

For all these reasons, the John Muir Trail section of the PCT is usually crowded in the summertime.

Most of the landscape along this section of the PCT is near-alpine forest, featuring several cold-tolerant kinds of

The photographer of this picture was lucky enough to accompany two great naturalists on a walk. On the left is John Burroughs and John Muir is on the right.

"Climb the mountains and get their good tidings. Nature's peace will flow into you as sunshine flows into trees. The winds will blow their own freshness into you, and the storms their energy, while cares will drop off like autumn leaves."

JOHN MUIR,
My First Summer in the Sierra

John Muir (1838–1914) worked hard to convince the U.S. government to protect the West's most scenic wilderness areas. His efforts led to the founding of national parks and other protected areas over hundreds of millions of acres—including Yosemite National Park. His writings continue to move, teach, and inspire nature lovers today.

pine trees, mountain hemlock, and a stunning assortment of mountain wildflowers. A few high-altitude passes are above timberline—higher than any trees can grow. In these alpine areas, only scruffy shrubs and smaller plants survive.

Summer comes late to these mountains. Even in May and June, there's usually a lot of snow on the ground. Hikers during snow season need good compass-and-map skills to find their way in the snow. Every snow-country hiker should also carry an ice axe, and know how to use it to stop uncontrolled slides down icy mountainsides.

Snowmelt brings a new danger in the High Sierra: The melting snow trickles down the mountainsides and gathers together in swollen, fast-moving creeks and rivers. Crossing these creeks when the water is high and fast can be dangerous.

Avalanche!

Avalanches happen when separately fallen layers of snow don't stick together, and the top layers slide downhill over the icy lower layers. An avalanche can be as small as a few yards wide—or as big as a mile wide, with tons of snow burying everything in its path.

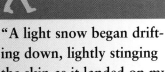

"A light snow began drifting down, lightly stinging the skin as it landed on my face; a world of granite, snow, and water.

"But as I trudged on, I heard a faint ticking sound near my feet. There was a tiny bird, puffed into a ball the size of an egg, pecking on a solid rock. What a tough guy. I knelt down right next to it to watch, and it didn't mind me a bit. Eventually it flew away; but that tiny, soft ball of life was an inspiration."

THRU-HIKER
TOM MARSHBURN

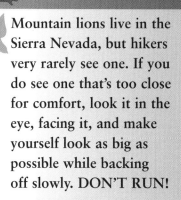

Mountain lions live in the Sierra Nevada, but hikers very rarely see one. If you do see one that's too close for comfort, look it in the eye, facing it, and make yourself look as big as possible while backing off slowly. DON'T RUN!

Like housecats, mountain lions like to chase running prey.

Mountain lion attacks on people are so rare that you're much more likely to be struck by lightning. If you are attacked, though— fight back!

A mountain lion, also known as a puma

> "Tuolumne Meadows . . . marauding bears ate three potscrubbers and my Guinness Book of World Records. . . . They even made an attempt on a can of motorcycle oil."
>
> THRU-HIKER
> DAVID GREEN

> "I sit . . . watching marmots that now come out of their holes to investigate us. A half dozen pop out to lie in the sun. They look like large groundhogs but sport long, bushy tails. Fat and clumsy, with yellow-brown fur, they're the only color in this stark [mountaintop] environment."
>
> THRU-HIKER
> CINDY ROSS

Danger walks with extraordinary beauty in the High Sierra. Hikers heading north along the PCT from Mount Whitney are treated to a unique string of beauty spots—quiet forests, sunny meadows, icy peaks.

Tuolumne Meadows to Sonora Pass

Beyond Tuolumne Meadows, the PCT leaves the John Muir Trail and follows along the Tuolumne River for a bit. Then the Trail zigzags northeast through Yosemite National Park. Here the Trail goes up and down (and up and down again and again) one deep, glacier-scraped canyon after another. Along the way, most summertime hikers make a short detour off the Trail to the sandy beach along the north shore of big Benson Lake. Ahead lies more up-and-downing, beautiful little ponds, and knockout views.

Water: Good Enough to Drink?

Water from even the cleanest-looking streams and lakes anywhere along the Trail can infect you with microscopic bugs that can make you feel like you've got stomach flu—or worse. For safe drinking water along the Trail you can: 1) carry enough clean drinking water with you, or 2) carry along water treatment pills or drops, or a specially made water filter, to kill whatever bugs might be growing in open water along the Trail.

"I got the Bad Water
   Blues,
The Bad Water Blues,
   that's so.
Well, my grits slip through
   my system
Like they slidin' down a
   greased flagpole."
                    THRU-HIKER
                    DAVID GREEN

Toward the northern end of this section, the Trail begins to cross more and more mountains capped long ago by volcanoes. There's lots more volcanic landscape ahead.

36

Northern SIERRA

Hikers along the Pacific Crest Trail's 270-mile (435-kilo-meter) route through the Northern Sierra travel through a landscape made mostly by volcanoes and erosion. Long ago, lava bubbled out of volcanoes here. The liquid rock turned solid as it cooled, in many places creating weird and wonderful shapes. Over time, erosion (wearing away) by glaciers and wind and water has remodeled the soft volcanic rock, creating the landscape PCT hikers see in the Northern Sierra today.

Sonora Pass to Echo Lake Resort

This section of the Trail starts out up-and-downing across a series of steep gullies at about 10,000 feet (3,048 meters) above sea level. In some spots, patches of snow linger as late as July. Past Sonora Peak, the Trail heads northwest down the East Fork Carson River Canyon. You've dropped below 10,000 feet here—and the north-

Hardened lava in the form of both pumice stone and obsidian

bound PCT stays below 10,000 feet from here all the way to Canada.

The Trail continues northwest to Ebbetts Pass and some bizarre volcanic landscaping just beyond. It then swings northeast into the Mokelumne Wilderness, then northwest again toward Carson Pass. From Carson Pass, the Trail follows along near the Upper Truckee River to Echo Lake. In the winter, the sprawling Echo Lake Resort,

Where did the lakes go? Hot, tired hikers notice that there are fewer lakes and ponds along the Trail in the Northern Sierra than in the High Sierra. Most of the Sierran lakes were carved out by glaciers, and glaciers usually carve smoother channels (with fewer lake basins) down canyons made of soft volcanic rock. Also, rock formed by volcanoes is full of small holes, so water running into a basin made of volcanic rock will often soak right into the ground instead of collecting in a pool, as it does in the glacier-carved granite basins found in the High Sierra. Most of the lakes in the Northern Sierra section of the Trail are in basins carved out of the granite in places where there's no overlayer of volcanic rock.

near busy Highway 50, is closed. In the summertime hiking season, the resort will accept and hold packages of supplies mailed to hikers.

Echo Lake Resort to Donner Pass

Beyond Echo Lake, the PCT swings northwest into Desolation Wilderness, keeping only a few miles away from the shores of busy Lake Tahoe. You can see Lake Tahoe, far below, from many places along the PCT here. Desolation Wilderness has plenty of lakes, but in many places few trees. Thousands of years ago, glaciers in this area not only carved out lake basins but also scraped away a lot of soil. In many places, there's just not enough soil to support trees. Desolation Wilderness is easy to reach and very popular with hikers, so it's often crowded in the summertime.

The crowds thin out farther north along the Trail. Beyond Barker Pass, the Trail enters Granite Chief Wilderness. There are some terrific views of Lake Tahoe and the mountains all around along the Trail here. The Trail continues northwest to Donner Pass.

Donner Pass to Sierra City

This short section of the Trail—only 38.4 miles (62 kilometers)—is easy to reach for a weekend hike, since there's a highway and nearby parking at both ends. For twenty-some miles, the Trail here runs north along a volcanic ridge where hikers can see for miles. The Trail then drops down to Jackson Meadow Reservoir, follows along rushing Milton Creek, and crosses the North Yuba River.

The Donner Party

There is an interstate highway at Donner Pass today, and travel is easy. In the past, though, getting through the pass was difficult and dangerous. In the winter of 1846–1847, a group of eighty-seven travelers (called the Donner party, after the family name of many of the travelers) tried to get over the Sierra on their way west. They got stuck in the snow near what is now called Donner Pass. They ran out of food, and before they were rescued some members of the group were so desperately hungry that they actually *ate* fellow travelers. Only half of the Donner party survived.

The forest here is mostly white fir. Northbound hikers will have seen a lot of white fir already at the higher altitudes south of here along the PCT. But here, at about 4,500 to 5,500 feet (1,300 to 1,600 meters) above sea level, sharp-eyed hikers will also notice more and more trees that do better at lower altitudes: incense cedar, sugar pine, ponderosa pine, Douglas fir, black oak.

Sierra City to Belden

Just past Sierra City, the PCT heads into the scenic Sierra Buttes. A steep side trail here leads to a long, rickety-looking, ladderlike stairway up, up, up to a fire lookout that hangs off a rocky peak. (Look down through the lookout platform's iron grating, and you'll see that you're hanging over a 600-foot (183-meter) drop!) Brave hikers who make this gut-busting and scary climb are rewarded with outstanding views of the great scenery all around.

Back on the Trail, hikers head northwest past Lakes Basin—a lot like Desolation Wilderness, but smaller, and seen at a distance from the Trail far above. The Trail con-

Near Pilot Peak: "As I came out of the forest to an exposed hill, [the storm] broke. The black clouds had reached my ridge, and a freezing wind whipped over the top. My hands, face, and legs went numb, and then sleet and hail began to patter around me.

"I virtually ran over the next bare hills until I found a spot with trees and, under my tarp, donned every piece of clothing I had in my pack. The hail made a loud but pleasant pattering, and feeling dry and warm, I ate lunch and read . . . while sitting by my pack under the tarp on a big tree root.

"The change was incredible. I had on mittens, hat, everything, whereas minutes before I had been hiking in my shorts. I can see how some people can freeze by failing to plan for bad weather."

THRU-HIKER
TOM MARSHBURN

tinues northwest past Mount Gibralter, and farther along past Pilot Peak. A little farther along, Chimney Rock—an easy-to-climb chunk of volcanic rock—juts out of the ground on top of a ridge.

The Trail crosses Middle Fork Feather River on a long arch bridge. This is an official "Wild and Scenic River Area" with wonderful pools in the river good for swimming, and warm, flat rocks good for sunbathing. Farther ahead, the Trail swings north around Bucks Lake toward Spanish Peak, then northwest past Mount Pleasant toward the small town of Belden. From the Trail's high point on Mount Pleasant—6,710 feet (2,045 meters) above sea level—to Belden—2,310 feet (704 meters)—hikers pass through several different plant communities adapted to these different altitudes—from red fir and western white pine on the mountain slopes to bay trees and live oaks near the river flowing through Belden.

42

Northern CALIFORNIA

Leaving behind the mighty Sierra Nevada, the north-bound Pacific Crest Trail still has more than 400 miles (644 kilometers) to go in California. It's usually hot and humid during hiking season here, with little rain from mid-June to September.

Belden to Burney Falls

The top scenic feature along this section of the Trail is volcanic Lassen Peak, 10,457 feet (3,187 meters) above sea level, the southernmost volcano in the Cascade Mountains. (The PCT will follow along or near the Cascades north all the way to Canada.) While the Trail swings well east of Lassen Peak and doesn't actually climb it, there are plenty of other things to see near the Trail in Lassen Volcanic National Park. Volcanic action underground here fuels bubbling hot springs, mudpots, geysers (hot water shooting out of the earth), and fumaroles (holes in the ground with steam coming out).

North of the Lassen Peak area, the Trail heads away from the park's evergreen forest and runs along the hot,

Near Mount Lassen: "The trail is strewn with pumice [a kind of volcanic rock]. I pick up one rock and am amazed at its slight weight. Then I notice that it is riddled with holes, which look like popped bubbles. And that's what they were—bubbles of gas trapped in the molten rock. . . .

"At Boiling [Springs] Lake . . . the water is a creamy mint green with orange and red earth surrounding it. . . . We see that the lake is, indeed, boiling, farting, belching, and smelling like rotten eggs. Mud pots along the shore spit and gurgle like bubbling porridge."

THRU-HIKER CINDY ROSS

dry, mostly shadeless Hat Creek Rim. In 1992, part of the PCT along Hat Creek Rim was moved to give thirsty hikers better access to drinking water. But there's still a 30-mile (48-kilometer) stretch of the Trail here without any drinkable water sources at all. This forces hikers to carry *gallons* of water to drink along the way. Adding to the misery, there are rattlesnakes aplenty, and zillions of sharp, pointy weed seeds that stick to hikers' socks and shoes.

Burney Falls to Castle Crags

Just off the Trail at the beginning of this section, Burney Falls is a thundering 130-foot (40-meter) waterfall fed by an underground lake. An average 200 million gallons (750 million liters) of water goes over the falls daily.

Beyond Burney Falls, the Trail winds west through thickly wooded mountains. Loggers cut down and haul away a lot of trees in this area, and hikers along the Trail here often hear the sounds of chainsaws and logging trucks.

The rocks underfoot at the beginning of this section were spewed out and spread around by volcanoes "only"

44

Burney Falls

a few million years ago. As you go up the Trail, though, the rocks underfoot are older. Beyond Grizzly Peak, some are 400 million years old.

Here and there along the Trail, hikers catch glimpses of magnificent Mount Shasta—14,162 feet (4,317 meters) above sea level—to the north, off the Trail. This enormous snow-capped volcano isn't dead, just dormant (resting). If it erupts again, lava flows and fiery ash could wipe out lots of towns on the mountainside and in the Sacramento River valley below.

45

Castle Crags to Etna Summit

This section starts off at dramatic Castle Crags, a mountain-sized chunk of granite-type rock sticking up out of the surrounding volcanic landscape.

Glaciers have stripped away a lot of volcanic rock in this section, leaving many little lake basins

The appropriately named Castle Crags

46

"That night I heard my friends the coyotes. They were in a frenzy: not mournful yipping, but a crazed chorus of yelps and barks, like hysterical laughter. Cowbells also sounded, so maybe a herd of cattle was being terrorized by coyotes. I rested a little uneasily, thinking of a cattle stampede through my meadow."

> THRU-HIKER
> TOM MARSHBURN

"I took the saddle off Fatima, and when I stepped backwards to put it under a tree, a large rattlesnake showed its presence *nearly* under our feet, coiling into a hot bundle of defense, rattling a warning that needs no explanation."

> LONG-DISTANCE
> HORSEBACK RIDER
> HAWK GREENWAY

Sixteen-year-old Hawk Greenway and his horse Fatima trekked along the PCT from northern California through Oregon and much of Washington one summer.

in the harder, granite-type rock below. The PCT passes right by three of these lakes. Several dozen more can be found a short walk off the Trail.

As in the previous section, there's lots of forest here—and lots of logging. In most places the Trail has been carefully routed away from the logging, to give hikers the feeling that they're in a real wilderness.

The Trail zigzags west and north, skirting the Trinity Alps Wilderness and passing through the Russian Wilderness on the way to Etna Summit, a mountain pass with a highway through it near the peak of Mount Etna.

"After I was asleep the deer came out. I awoke several times to loud whuffing sounds of the deer blasting air through their nostrils. If I moved, their hooves would crack against the rock as they ran. Sounded like gun-shots."

THRU-HIKER
TOM MARSHBURN

A deer at rest
on the trail

Etna Summit to Seiad Valley

From Etna Summit, the Trail continues north, skimming from one mountain ridge to another, crossing the canyons in between at high points in the Marble Mountain Wilderness. The highlights along the Trail in this wilderness area are Black Mountain, Kings Castle, and Marble Mountain. (A half-hour side trip takes you to the top of Marble Mountain. You can see most of northwestern California from there.)

"I descended on towards Cook and Green Pass. Whistling and rounding a corner, I could hear some rustling and breaking of twigs. A deer, I thought.

It was a bear. A big black bear, twenty feet from me. I froze. I couldn't do anything. My heart was about to jump up my throat. The bear took little notice of me, and he slowly turned his head in my direction. He was tearing up a tree, his feet wrapped around the trunk, his back to me. He saw me, blinked, rose up on his haunches, and dove down the slope, his body shaking and swerving as he ran; and then all I could see was dust and the tops of little trees come wrenching down, and all I could hear was a sound like thunder or a freight train. The ground shook."

THRU-HIKER
TOM MARSHBURN

Beyond Marble Mountain Wilderness, the Trail drops down through a Douglas fir-lined canyon holding Grider Creek. Grider Creek (and the PCT) eventually run into the much bigger Klamath River and a road. The Trail follows paved road for a few miles to a bridge over the river, and then to the small town of Seiad Valley.

Seiad Valley to the California/Oregon Border

Beyond Seiad Valley, the Trail jogs east along the crests of thickly wooded Siskiyou mountain ridges. Much of the Trail runs near logging roads here.

The reason for this long eastward jog is so the Trail can rejoin the Cascade Mountains. The Trail curved west

Bigfoot! Sasquatch! Yeti! In the forests and canyons of the Siskiyous, dozens of people have reported seeing what they thought was a Sasquatch—a tall, hairy, humanlike creature.

"Although there is no proof that the Sasquatch exists, every hiker who passes through these mountains must wonder, as we did, about whether there is any truth to the legend. I walked with sharp eyes, alert ears, and my camera at the ready—without results."

THRU-HIKER
CINDY ROSS

of the Cascades back near Mount Shasta, to avoid some long dry stretches.

Midway through this eastward trek, between Ward's Fork Gap and Jackson Gap (in the middle of nowhere), northbound hikers on the Trail at long last cross over the state border from California into Oregon. By the time they reach this border, thru-hikers who started at the Mexican border have walked more than 1,700 miles (2,700 kilometers)!

OREGON

The Pacific Crest Trail continues its northward march up the Cascade Mountains through Oregon. The top two Trail highlights in Oregon are both awesomely huge: Crater Lake and Mount Hood. July and August are the warmest, least rainy, and most popular months for hiking along the Trail in Oregon.

California / Oregon Border to Crater Lake

From the state border, the PCT continues its eastward swing through heavily logged forest to rejoin the Cascade mountain range. Long-distance hikers who get through this not-very-scenic stretch are rewarded for their patience when the Trail heads north into Sky Lakes Wilderness. Here, hikers along the Trail pass through forested wilderness mostly unchanged by human activities. There's great swimming in many mountain lakes along or near the Trail here.

Heading north, the Trail leaves Sky Lakes Wilderness and enters Crater Lake National Park. A different name,

"As I left the road behind, a peaceful feeling came over me. I found myself in silence, leading the calm Fatima behind me. I began to really see the land I was passing through—the way the oak and fir trees fit into the swales and gulleys of the hillside. The trail traversed the hill, crossing meadows of sun-cured grass. There was a deer sleeping under the trees, a hawk cruising overhead, wind (or was it mice?) rustling the tall grass. I felt the coolness of the fir trees' shade, the heat of the open slope."

LONG-DISTANCE
HORSEBACK RIDER
HAWK GREENWAY

but the woodsy scenery is much the same. The Trail here runs for several miles along the rim of the famous lake that gives the park its name.

Crater Lake

Crater Lake fills the huge hole created by a volcano that erupted here, where Mount Mazama used to be, some 7,000 years ago. When it erupted, Mount Mazama spit out enormous quantities of volcanic smoke, ash, and other debris with such force that it spread over thousands of square miles. The volcano also burped up countless tons of lava. So much melted rock burbled out that the mountaintop emptied and collapsed in on itself, leaving only a huge caldera (volcanic hole) 6 miles (9.6 kilometers) wide. In time, this crater filled with rain and snowmelt, becoming Crater Lake.

Today, a road runs along the rim of Crater Lake. Hordes of tourists visit Rim Drive each year to stare over the crater's edge into the deep blue waters of the lake, 1,000 feet (305 meters) or more below the rim. Yes, this *is* the bluest lake you've ever seen. Its color looks so vivid because the water is so deep—1,932 feet (589 meters)—and because the viewpoints along the rim are so high above the water.

Crater Lake to Mount Hood

Back on the Trail, hikers continue north through the Cascades into Mount Thielsen Wilderness. Most hikers make a short (but awfully steep) side trip to the top of Mount Thielsen—9,182 feet (2,799 meters). In addition to a great view of Crater Lake from the peak of Mount

An aerial view of Crater Lake and the cinder cone called Wizard Island

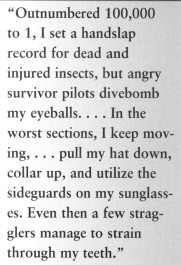

Thielsen, on a clear day you can see all the way south to Mount Shasta, 120 miles (193 kilometers) away, and north to Mount Jefferson, 107 miles (172 kilometers) away.

Beyond Mount Thielsen Wilderness, the PCT winds through Diamond Peak Wilderness northward into Three Sisters Wilderness. The middle of Three Sisters Wilderness, dotted with lovely little lakes, is famous for its ferocious mosquitoes. Farther north, the Trail climbs up higher into the mountains, away from the worst of the mosquitoes. In this very popular hiking area, the Trail skirts the western slopes of the scenic "Sisters" mountains: South Sister, Middle Sister, and North Sister. (The Trail also passes by peaks named The Wife and The Husband.)

After crossing over a state highway at McKenzie Pass, the Trail continues north through Mount Washington Wilderness and Mount Jefferson Wilderness. The highlights along the Trail here are three more scenic mountains: Mount Washington, Three Fingered Jack, and Mount Jefferson. Like the Sisters to the south, these mountains are old volcanoes that have been eroded by wind, water, and glaciers.

Mount Hood to the Oregon/Washington Border

North of Barlow Pass, the PCT enters Mount Hood Wilderness. On the southern slopes of Mount Hood, the Trail passes Timberline Lodge. This large, rustic, and very grand hotel was built as a government-sponsored work

Timberline Lodge, with a view of Mount Jefferson in the distance

project during the Great Depression of the 1930s. Today, it's a popular vacation spot for skiers as well as hikers.

Mount Hood, 11,235 feet (3,424 meters) above sea level, is *always* covered with snow. Each year's snowfall adds a little more to the glaciers that flow down its sides—just like the glaciers that covered so much of North America long ago, during the last Ice Age. But these glaciers aren't about to cover Oregon. As they move downhill from the icy mountaintop, they run into warmer weather. In the summertime, a lot of glacial ice melts, feeding countless little streams running down the mountain. Summertime melting roughly equals wintertime snowfall, so the glaciers don't grow or shrink very much.

"Rain washes the mountains and intensifies with alarming speed. . . . Lightning leapfrogs from cloud to cloud, cleaving the skies. A thunderbolt spirals down an isolated tree trunk. . . .

"This light show ignites over 40 fires in the area. Sheets of yellow flame lap at downed logs like unfurled flags flapping in the wind. This sucking inferno crackles in the trees. . . . A horrendous roar literally dances down the slopes."

THRU-RUNNER
BOB HOLTEL

Fires started by lightning are a natural part of the forest and dryland ecosystems along the PCT. A normal fire in a healthy forest will leave many of the big trees alive while burning up thick undergrowth. This makes room for a new generation of plants to grow. These once-in-a-while fires prevent too much dead wood from piling up to fuel a truly terrible fire that would kill everything in its path.

Summertime melting often causes avalanches and rockslides on Mount Hood. Only experienced and well-equipped mountain climbers should even try to reach its peak. Many mountaineers who do attempt it make their climb at night, reaching the peak at sunrise so they can get down off the icy slopes before the sun starts another day of dangerous melting.

Most hikers don't climb Mount Hood. Many hikers do, however, detour from the PCT to take a long day's hike on a side trail that circles the mountain at about timberline. Cold as it is here, it's very hot deep underfoot; Mount Hood is, after all, a volcano. And it's not dead, only resting. Like many of its neighboring mountains, Mount Hood will likely erupt again some day.

"We run down the hill behind the shelter and there, across a boggy meadow, stand the long-legged golden animals. Big. Much bigger than deer. We sneak along the edge of the trees, still a good distance away, trying for a closer view. . . . A bull elk raises its massive rack [of antlers] and looks our way with stern, dark eyes. In a matter of seconds, the whole herd thunders away."

THRU-HIKER
CINDY ROSS

A bull moose gathers his herd together.

The Columbia River Gorge

Beyond Mount Hood Wilderness, the Trail drops through thick, lush, moist Oregon forest in the Columbia Wilderness to the mighty Columbia River. Over thousands of years, the river has cut a deep channel, called a gorge, through the Cascade Mountains. The deep, steep walls of the Columbia River gorge are thickly covered with forest kept moist and lush year-round by misty, rainy breezes rolling in from the Pacific Ocean.

57

Hiking toward Mount Hood: "If you don't lift your head to see Mount Hood's bulk rising in the sky, and if you ignore the fact that you're climbing, you would think that you were transported to a beach somewhere. Grasses grow long and wild and wave in the wind on Mount Hood's south side. Your boots sink three inches into the soft, gray sand, and you're tempted to go barefoot."

THRU-HIKER CINDY ROSS

"Today [along the trail] was a fine day for 'deep-forest relaxing,' that feeling that comes when I travel on trails covered with fir needles and where there are quiet springs bubbling out from under tree roots. I very much enjoyed being alone today, just letting my mind wander where it would, not worrying much at all."

LONG-DISTANCE
HORSEBACK RIDER
HAWK GREENWAY

The Columbia River itself used to be home to literally millions of wild salmon. Now hydroelectric dams along the river have made it much more difficult for salmon to make their way upstream to spawn. There are far fewer fish in the river than there used to be. The dams along this powerful river generate huge amounts of electricity for western cities.

The northbound PCT drops down to the south bank of the Columbia River. Near the river, hikers pass the lowest spot on the entire Trail—only 140 feet (43 meters) above sea level. The Trail crosses under the busy freeway leading west to Portland, then crosses the Columbia River into Washington on the old steel Bridge of the Gods.

WASHINGTON

In cool, rainy Washington, the Pacific Crest Trail climbs north from the mighty Columbia River up to the lower slopes of magnificent Mount Rainier, then on past one glacier-covered peak after another to the Trail's end at the Canadian border.

Columbia River to Mount Rainier

From its lowest point near the Columbia River, the Trail climbs sharply back up into the Cascade Mountains. In summertime, PCT hikers can enjoy plenty of ripe, delicious wild huckleberries here. In some places, though, signs say that the berries are reserved for Indians only, by agreement with the U.S. government. Native Americans from as far away as Montana have been coming here for centuries to pick and dry the berries.

"We edge around a two-foot long, brownish-black porcupine . . . on a sharp turn. Its back and tail are covered with strong, stiff quills. When defending themselves, their barbed tips penetrate flesh like miniature darts. . . . Once around we move on."

THRU-RUNNER
BOB HOLTEL

A porcupine. They won't bother you if you don't bother them.

A little more than 100 miles (161 kilometers) from the Trail's lowest point, hikers reach its highest point in Washington—7,080 feet (2,158 meters) above sea level. Along the way, the Trail passes through several different ecosystems: from the moist forest of the Columbia River gorge, past lakes set in old lava fields scraped by glaciers, through scruffy and cold-tolerant near-alpine forest, to the alpine landscape near Packwood Glacier in the Goat Rocks Wilderness. (The Trail actually cuts across part of this glacier.)

While huffing and puffing up this long climb, hikers from time to time see not only big Mount Adams, 12,307 feet (3,751 meters) above sea level, just to the east of the

While taking a breather for munchies and liquid, I search out a flat log to stretch out on. Behind it lies a tiny, quivering fawn, still slightly wet from its recent birth. Huddled in an almost fetal position like a ball of mottled, spotted fur, it is sleepy-eyed and nearly motionless except for visible fright.

"A quiet chill of excitement moves up my spine. I try to be discreet with my quick stares, gazing only as long as I dare. Its outsized ears lay back flat against its head. The spots on its back are . . . off-white, perfectly blended into a background of milk chocolate brown. Twice it cocks its head for signs of danger. I could barely distinguish several sighs and soft grunts before it curls up and goes back to sleep."

THRU-RUNNER
BOB HOLTEL

Trail, but also the recently active volcano Mount St. Helens, a few miles west of the Trail. In 1980, Mount St. Helens erupted violently, spitting smoke and millions of tons of ash hundreds of miles around. (The Mount St. Helens eruption was big news, but as volcanic eruptions go, it was only so-so. The volcanic eruption that created Crater Lake was about 40 times more powerful than the show Mount St. Helens put on.)

North of Goat Rocks, the Trail winds through near-alpine wilderness near where three parklands meet: William O. Douglas Wilderness (named after Supreme Court Justice Douglas, a great lover and protector of America's natural landscapes), Norse Peak Wilderness, and Mount Rainier National Park. The land along the Trail here gets lots of rain, so below timberline are deep, dark, quiet groves of towering evergreens.

61

Mount Rainier to the Canadian Border

The PCT doesn't actually climb mighty Mount Rainier. Instead, the Trail swings about 12 miles (19 kilometers) to the east of Rainier's glacier-covered peak. At 14,410 feet (4,392 meters) above sea level, Mount Rainier's peak is the highest in the Cascade Mountains. Its system of glaciers is larger than any other single mountain's glaciers in all of North America except Alaska.

North of the Norse Peak Wilderness, the Trail drops down out of the near-alpine zone into a warmer mountain forest. With no "wilderness zone" protection, much of this forest has been cut down for lumber.

At Snoqualmie Pass, the Trail crosses busy Interstate 90—the road to Seattle. Beyond lies some challenging up-and-downing past more glacier-covered peaks. This far north, the Trail is usually blocked by snow well into July! Even in August, the warmest month, snow lingers in many places along the Trail. Where the snow is melted, dazzling mountain wildflowers are in bloom. The growing season is so short here that all the flowers seem to bloom at once, racing to set seed before the snow comes again.

North of Castle Pass, the Trail approaches Monument 78. This miniature bronze "Washington Monument," not quite 5 feet (1.5 meters) tall, marks the border between the United States and Canada. But it's not quite the end of the PCT. The Trail continues a few short miles into Canada, to Route 3. Hikers who have stayed with the Trail all the way from Mexico to Canada are finally at their journey's end—more than 2,600 miles (4,184 km) after they started!

he Pacific Crest Trail is managed and kept in shape by various government agencies and by thousands of volunteers working all along the Trail. If you want to help keep the Trail in good condition—or if you just want to know more about it—write or call:

Pacific Crest Trail Association
5325 Elkhorn Blvd., Suite 256
Sacramento, CA 95842
1-888-PC-TRAIL

The hiker's quotes in *Step By Step Along the Pacific Crest Trail* were found in these books:

Green, David. *A Pacific Crest Odyssey: Walking the Trail from Mexico to Canada.* Berkeley, California: Wilderness Press, 1979.

Greenway, Hawk. *The Trail North: A Solo Journey on the Pacific Crest.* Covelo, California: Island Press, 1981.

Holtel, Bob. *Soul, Sweat, and Survival on the Pacific Crest Trail.* Livermore, California: Bittersweet Publishing Company, 1994.

Jardine, Ray. *The PCT Hiker's Handbook: Innovative Techniques and Trail Tested Instruction for the Long Distance Backpacker.* LaPine Oregon: AdventureLore Press, 1992.

Marshburn, Tom. *Six-Moon Trail: Canada to Mexico Along the Pacific. Crest.* Pasadena, California: Robert K. Leishman, 1986.

Ross, Cindy. *Journey on the Crest: Walking 2600 Miles From Mexico to Canada.* Seattle: The Mountaineers, 1987.

Ryback, Eric. *The High Adventure of Eric Ryback: Canada to Mexico on Foot.* San Francisco: Chronicle Books, 1971.

INDEX

Page numbers in *italics* refer to illustrations.